Today I Will Indulge My Inner Glutton

ANN THORNHILL & SARAH WELLS

Today I Will Indulge My Inner Glutton

HEALTH-FREE AFFIRMATIONS FOR CYNICS

PRIMA PUBLISHING

PRIMA PUBLISHING and colophon are registered trademarks of Prima Communications, Inc.

Library of Congress Cataloging-in-Publication Data

Thornhill, Ann.
    Today I will indulge my inner glutton : health-free affirmations for cynics / Ann Thornhill and Sarah Wells.
        p. cm.
    ISBN 0-7615-2109-7
    1. Affirmations Humor. 2. Human behavior Humor. 3. Body, Human Humor.
    4. Health Humor. I. Wells, Sarah. II. Title.
PN6231.H38T46 1999
818'.5402—dc21
                                                                                    99-34386
                                                                                    CIP

99 00 01 02 HH 10 9 8 7 6 5 4 3 2 1
Printed in the United States of America

HOW TO ORDER

Single copies may be ordered from Prima Publishing, P.O. Box 1260BK, Rocklin, CA 95677; telephone (916) 632-4400. Quantity discounts are also available. On your letterhead, include information concerning the intended use of the books and the number of books you wish to purchase.

Visit us online at www.primalifestyles.com

This book is dedicated to
all of our much loved family and friends.
Their glaring personal flaws inspired us
and made this book just that much easier to write.
Thanks to each and every one of you.

*I*n a world where appearance is everything, this book is for those few courageous souls who are brave enough to be unattractive and socially repugnant. Rather than applauding the simple manifestation of superior genes, we choose to celebrate the daily practice and dogged persistence of unsightly looks and unseemly behavior. It's high time we reclaim such words as *smelly* and *gross!*

Or, on those days when we do feel like chasing the dream of beauty, it's time we realize we have every right to beg, borrow, steal, and sabotage in order to do so.

So, come on, join us in a revolt. Let's finally

recognize the stupidity of gyms, or let's at least accept that we will be poor sports when we get there. Go ahead, embrace those imperfections, or, depending on the day, try to stamp them all out. It's your choice.

$\mathcal{T}$oday I will intentionally tell a coworker whom I dislike and who has obviously gained weight that she is looking thin.

$\mathcal{T}$oday I will embrace my shallow existence.

$\mathcal{I}$f I could just surround myself with sycophants, I would never have to deal with who I really am and how I really look.

෧ඏ

$\mathcal{I}$f I could only allow others to touch me, then I'm sure I would enjoy a massage.

$\mathcal{I}$n order to feel productive today,
I will go on a ludicrous fad diet that
will accomplish nothing except make
me miserable.

$\mathcal{T}$oday I will direct all my resentment
towards people who can afford
personal trainers.

$\mathcal{I}$ understand that I must learn to love my body, but I reserve the right to do so only when highly medicated.

$\mathcal{I}$f we could harness the energy created when my thighs rub together, not only would it save the environment, but it would make me a hero.

So that I can let go of my negative thoughts, I will begin to voice them out loud no matter where I am or who I'm with.

Today I will "accidentally" knock over all the really good-looking people in my aerobics class so that they cannot return, and I can finally be at ease.

In order to kill two birds with one stone, I will spend all this week's food allowance on an extremely expensive wrinkle cream.

☙☙

Today I will pretend that the swoosh of my corduroy-clad thighs chafing together is actually the stirring soundtrack to a movie of which I am the star.

$\mathcal{T}$oday I will indulge my inner glutton.

෧ඉ

$\mathcal{I}$nstead of going out with friends this evening, I'll stay home and create an elaborate montage of old photographs so that I can more quickly and effectively depress myself.

$\mathcal{I}$ have a right to deny my ever-expanding girth by purchasing only clothes with elastic waistbands.

$\mathcal{I}$ celebrate my bodily deformities.

$\mathcal{I}$ accept that I have childbearing hips which, unfortunately, seem to be geared towards the birth of a nation.

$\mathcal{T}$oday I will obsess over the correct way to eradicate my ever-increasing facial hair.

Today I will remind myself that one's metabolism slows down as one ages. Therefore, it is better for me to pig out tonight than tomorrow night.

Today I will paste cut-out pictures of supermodels on all the fattening containers of food in my house. I will then imagine them whispering "piggy" when I reach for those cartons.

$\mathcal{T}$oday I will test my doctor's intelligence by combining the symptoms of four deadly diseases and see if she catches on.

$\mathcal{T}$oday I will purchase a shockingly bad toupee or wig in the hopes that no one will notice the rest of my appearance.

$\mathcal{T}$oday I will purposely wear clothes with stains all over them so that people will pity me.

෧෨

$\mathcal{B}$ecause I hate how busy I am at work, I will rise to new heights of incompetence by perfecting my slovenly appearance.

$\mathcal{M}$y excessive caffeine
consumption allows me to play
pranks on people in the middle of
the night.

$\mathcal{W}$henever I am out in public,
I prefer to have small splatters of
food on my clothes rather than huge
wet spots.

In order to recapture my youth,
no matter how ridiculous I may look,
today I will wear styles befitting a
teenager.

I like the fact that my shirts gap in
the front because I get to show my
otherwise hidden, pretty camisoles.

$\mathcal{A}$s long as I surround myself with older and larger people, I can realistically remain younger and thinner.

❧

$\mathcal{R}$ather than keeping my stress bottled up inside, today I will loudly announce my anguish to the world.

Today when I see a jogger I will remind myself that I have a more effective mode of transportation . . . a car.

Today I will support my inner sloth.

Although I'd love to get a tattoo, this year's cute little doggie would most likely grow into next year's Godzilla as my body expands.

When I was young, I searched for shapes in the clouds. Because that particular game is for children, I will refine it by looking for shapes in my spider veins.

$\mathcal{J}$udging by my physical appearance, my parents were either genetic anomalies or closely related.

∾

$\mathcal{T}$he next time I'm at a family reunion, I will be very rude to all my relatives who so cruelly gave me these physical traits.

When I swim, the flapping, loose skin on the undersides of my arms makes my waves that much more definitive.

❧

My round, jolly appearance softens the sarcastic venom that often spews from my mouth.

Today I will make up false but gripping stories about how I acquired all of my scars.

I am the direct descendant of trolls and troglodytes.

When I get upset at my children,
I must remember to blame them for
how haggard I look.

Because I am so easily spiritually
isolated, I celebrate that my Buddha-
like appearance helps to bring me
closer to religion.

As part of a new diet plan, I will increase my fiber intake until my stomach cramps elicit sympathy from others.

I must remember this summer that overcooling my home allows me to avoid wearing revealing clothes.

Unlike the expensive, energy-consuming thrills of a roller coaster, I prefer the old-fashioned surge and fall of a sugar high.

My doctor's scale is apparently set on ounces.

$\mathcal{T}$oday, I will kindly and helpfully call my doctor again to remind him to get his scale checked.

$\mathcal{P}$lastic surgery can effectively accomplish what years of therapy cannot: self-acceptance.

$\mathcal{M}$y uncontrolled, periodic bodily noises add punctuation and importance to any conversation.

$\mathcal{N}$ot only is my big hair attractive, it puts me in another height/weight category.

$\mathcal{B}$ecause I hate conflict and so have not been able to break up with my lover, I will instead cleverly stop bathing and clipping my toenails.

$\mathcal{I}$ accept that medications are a more timely and efficient solution to my physical problems than exercise and diet could ever be.

In order to make people listen to me, today I will invade everyone's personal space.

Today, I will get back at all those nasty people who tried to get away from me yesterday by backing them into a wall.

I must remind myself that I now have the confidence to exact revenge on all the people who teased me as a child.

My large tummy conveniently eliminates the need for coffee tables and dinner trays.

My penchant for dying my hair drastic colors allows me to employ a technique similar to "carbon dating" when looking at old photos.

Although my life is outwardly boring, I have the private adventure of discovering new and bizarre growths on my skin.

$\mathcal{I}$n order to fulfill my unrealistic yearnings for a glamorous life and beautiful body, today I will pretend I am an actual movie star.

$\mathcal{B}$ecause exercise really sucks up my energy, today I will instead enroll my child in a sports team. That way I can remain comfortable as I watch others exercise.

Today I will pretend that everyone who stares at me is actually bewitched by my inherent grace and elegance.

Today I will begin conditioning my body to eat unhealthy foods. I will eat only foods that irritate my stomach and give me heartburn so that I can become accustomed to them.

So that I am no longer shocked by my appearance, I will install mirrors on every wall in my home.

This week I will pretend to be sick so that I can eat all my comfort foods.

$\mathcal{T}$oday I will call off work, saying that I'm having an ugly day and none of my clothes fit properly.

$\mathcal{I}$ think my twitches and tics are adorable expressions of my personality.

My habit of constantly furrowing my brow serves the dual purpose of making me look both intelligent and concerned.

෨෨

Today I will begin a top-secret investigation of all major food companies to prove that they used premature babies to determine their serving sizes.

$\mathcal{T}$oday I will celebrate the fact that my profile looks like Boris Karloff's.

$\mathcal{M}$y creaking joints allow me to add enthralling sound effects to all the stories I tell.

$\mathcal{M}$y ability to discuss extremely personal physical ailments with complete strangers proves I am comfortable with myself.

$\mathcal{M}$y outrageous comments and rude behavior allow me to go through life like a secret agent—no one remembers what I look like, just what I said.

$\mathcal{M}$y bizarre sleep habits allow me to acquaint myself with delightful, late-night TV programs.

$\mathcal{W}$henever my overly sensitive friends say I'm demanding, I remain anchored and secure in the knowledge that I'm helping them to be their best.

$\mathcal{T}$he next time someone remarks on the yellow underarm stains on all my shirts, I'll inform her that it's actually a subtle tie-dye technique.

$\mathcal{T}$oday I will encourage my imminent collapse.

Some folks complain about my clammy, weak handshake; I think it is a fine expression of my mediocre character.

Since I'm starting my three-day crash diet next week, I must remember to binge all this week.

This will be the year that I finally solve the mystery of how my off-season clothes shrink to children's sizes every year.

છ૭

My complete lack of impulse control proves that my needs are stronger than most people's.

$\mathcal{T}$oday I will take a large box of donuts to an Overeater's Anonymous meeting so that I can feel superior to everybody who eats one.

$\mathcal{I}$ don't understand all the hoopla about meditation, since a good, stiff drink does the exact same thing.

Since years of therapy haven't made me feel any less awkward, today I will resort to criticizing others as a cost-effective way to cheer myself up.

In order to justify my monk-like celibacy, today I will scare myself silly by reading all the free pamphlets on STDs at my doctor's office.

Out of respect for starving children everywhere, this year I will force myself to clean my plate—even if it sickens me.

So as to be a stranger to my present self, my New Year's resolution is to greet the end of the year with a completely new self on all levels—physical, emotional, psychological, and spiritual.

$\mathcal{I}$n order to be the center of attention at the gym today, I will "unveil" my personalized, made-up exercises.

$\mathcal{T}$oday I will finally allow myself to relax and have some free time. I will take a book to work and read all day.

The fact that my shadow looks like that of an NFL linebacker has probably saved me from many threatening situations.

Although the synthetic ingredients in the diet foods I subsist on may well be doing serious, long-term damage to my body, it is more important for me to be thin than healthy.

$\mathcal{I}$f people were more refined and
educated, they would then be able to
see how truly beautiful I am.

$\mathcal{T}$oday I will fuel someone's
self-doubt.

$\mathcal{M}$ost people simply do not have the depth of character to dress as freakishly as I do.

$\mathcal{I}$ am proud that I have a consistent, albeit unpleasant, personality.

$\mathcal{F}$inally, I am able to appreciate that the harsh glare from my excessively oily skin prevents people from taking photographs of me.

$\mathcal{N}$ot only do I have my mother's thighs, they seem to have adhered themselves to my own thighs.

$\mathcal{B}$ecause it's important for everyone to look their best, this year I will volunteer to do makeovers at a homeless shelter.

$\mathcal{I}$n order to draw attention away from the rest of my body, this year I will glue rhinestones and glitter on the neckline of all my clothes and shoes.

$\mathcal{M}$y complete lack of standards allows me to eat at any fast food restaurant.

$\mathcal{T}$oday I will practice covertly crossing my eyes and making goofy faces. When my uptight boss comments on it, I will explain that I'm simply getting used to my new bifocals.

$\mathcal{I}$ am convinced it would be easier for me to exercise if I was in better physical condition.

$\mathcal{A}$lthough I could selfishly do my own yard work, my philanthropic ideals force me to employ vagrants who are less fortunate than I.

$\mathcal{M}$y unusually large, flat feet help to counteract my unfortunate habit of toppling over.

$\mathcal{B}$ecause I have no passion for anything, I can more easily pretend to be enthralled by other people's petty diversions and activities.

$\mathcal{M}$y uneven breasts allow me to view the ground from two different perspectives.

$\mathcal{M}$y painful arthritis enables me to be lazy while simultaneously receiving attention from others.

$\mathcal{A}$lthough some say altruism can be beneficial to one's health, I believe that it interferes with my selfishness.

$\mathcal{T}$oday I will give all my coworkers articles I've found on the Internet that address their specific flaws and offer advice on how to fix them.

$\mathcal{T}$oday I will convince myself that my double chin is actually the beginning of a goiter.

∾

$\mathcal{T}$he severely uneven and dimpled surface of my cellulite transforms my boring, over-tight clothes into truly unique and highly textured designer look-alikes.

$\mathcal{G}$oals are for people who can't handle the spontaneity and unpredictability of life.

$\mathcal{I}$f I could stomach the thought of eating fruits and vegetables then I'm sure I could master the discipline of being a vegetarian.

In order to prevent osteoporosis, today I will eat lots of cheese, whipping cream, and ice cream.

I'm certain that when my doctor said I need to eat breakfast, she was overlooking the fact that I always have two cups of coffee and four cigarettes first thing in the morning.

$\mathcal{B}$ecause I am so out of touch with my body, I am able to cloak myself in many layers of clothing regardless of the temperature.

$\mathcal{A}$s it prevents the need for regular physicals, today I will celebrate my efficient use of hypochondria.

$\mathcal{S}$o that I don't have to develop my empathy skills, today I will point out the silver lining in every problem anyone tells me, no matter how dire.

$\mathcal{S}$ince I spend too much time agonizing over my own problems, today I will refresh myself by focusing on impending meteorological and geological disasters.

$\mathcal{B}$ecause I have no interest in addressing other people's needs, I will surround myself with others who only like me for my money.

$\mathcal{T}$he next time I go out to dinner with someone who is thinner than I am, I will persuade him to get a fattening dessert while I profess to be full. I will then look on judgmentally.

The next time someone asks me if I'm pregnant, I will kindly inform her that I'm actually providing a free, safe home to an endangered parasite.

This year I will make it a point to always be dressed in my finest clothes so that I don't get stuck changing a stranger's tire or helping a friend move.

$\mathcal{I}$ am certain I could adapt to changes more readily if I could control all aspects of them.

$\mathcal{J}$ ust because I tend to have humanly attainable expectations doesn't mean other people shouldn't at least try to meet them.

*I*f people don't want my opinion, they shouldn't make eye contact with me.

∞

I delight in the fact that no one, including myself, remembers what my true hair color is.

The next time my boss asks me a pesky question, I'll pretend I'm practicing my mime routine for dinner theater.

∞

Feelings are never right or wrong. Except mine.

$\mathcal{A}$lthough a lot of people call me spooky, I'm sure their petty minds simply cannot grasp the profound significance of my existence.

$\mathcal{M}$y inability to get along with others protects me from the dangers of cults.

$\mathcal{T}$he next time someone mentions
their mid-life crisis, I will politely
remind them that my life has been
one big crisis since the day I was born.

❧

$\mathcal{I}$t would be much easier for me to
develop my spirituality if it didn't
interfere with my consumerism.

$\mathcal{I}$n order to confuse people and deflect responsibility, I will respond to every accusation by arbitrarily making quote signs around chosen words.

$\mathcal{T}$oday I will cherish my internal critic.

In order to make everyone in my life as self-conscious as I am, I will give weight-loss books as birthday presents from now on.

Even though I am extremely unproductive, I deserve as much leisure time as a house cat.

Since I will never achieve
supermodel beauty, it is probably best
for me to never attempt to change
my physical appearance in any way.

Because it is common knowledge
that all new regimes work best when
started first thing Monday mornings,
if I feel like exercising before that,
I will force myself to wait.

$\mathcal{T}$oday I will remind myself to stop shrieking whenever I inadvertently catch sight of myself in a mirror.

৩৯

$\mathcal{I}$n order to come up with new and yet completely unrealistic self-improvement ideas, this week I will watch as much TV as possible, using only incredibly glamorous stars as role models.

$\mathcal{I}$ have a right to set my sights no higher than being the best slug-like life form that I can be.

$\mathcal{S}$ince I'm having trouble motivating myself to lose weight, I will resort to my old standbys: shame and judgment.

$\mathcal{I}$ like the fact that my dull, lifeless hair hangs over my face, obscuring my identity.

$\mathcal{A}$fter years of yo-yo dieting, I must recognize the fact that I have inadvertently lowered my daily caloric needs to seven.

$\mathcal{G}$iven my poor history of self-improvement, today I will remind myself that choice is just an illusion.

$\mathcal{B}$ecause I know what is best for everyone, instead of keeping a self-improvement journal I will keep a journal on how my friends could improve themselves.

The next time I have the urge to eat compulsively, I will distract myself by picking a fight with my most spineless friend.

∞

Today I will escalate my emotional turmoil.

Since I don't like to be around things that scare me, today I will practice having out-of-body experiences.

In order to make up for all the years I punished myself, today I will reward myself hourly and expensively.

$\mathcal{I}$n an effort to save myself precious time, I will start eating straight from the serving dish.

$\mathcal{I}$f visualization is the key to change, today I will visualize myself as a perfect being with no problems.

$\mathcal{T}$he next time I have a negative thought, I'll scream out "stop that" no matter where I am.

$\mathcal{T}$oday I will compare myself unfavorably to every person I see.

$\mathcal{I}$nstead of overeating when I am stressed, today I will resort to belittling others.

☙❧

$\mathcal{T}$oday I will falsify my weight on my doctor's chart so that the next time I go everyone will congratulate me on my stunning weight loss.

$\mathcal{B}$ecause I am terrified of my emotions, the only feeling I will allow myself today is hunger.

$\mathcal{S}$ince there are no safe people in my life, I will continue to confide only in my pets and complete strangers.

$\mathcal{M}$y inability to mature and grow guarantees me security in this changing and uncertain world.

$\mathcal{A}$lthough I've never been a smoker, today I will experiment with the nicotine patch in order to raise my energy level. Hopefully, it will push me into a drug-induced exercise mania.

$\mathcal{T}$oday I will agree to do something I don't want to do so later I can feel resentment towards the person who took advantage of me.

$\mathcal{S}$ince I often have trouble feeling completely present in any given situation, I will begin to announce my presence as a skillful grounding technique. "I am here" should work perfectly.

Today I will begin searching for a therapist who will help me clinically label my family and friends.

This week my therapist will help me project my problems onto my family and friends.

When that therapist begins to show her true nature, I will search for a new therapist to help me understand the evil and insidious needs of my prior therapist.

I'm sure if my problems were as petty as everyone else's, I could easily find a therapist with whom I could work.

Today I will celebrate the fact that my shame keeps me from looking as foolish as everyone else.

Today I will cheapen my inherent worth.

$\mathcal{I}$f my coworkers weren't so completely annoying, I wouldn't need three drinks to get me through the morning.

$\mathcal{I}$ accept the fact that my body, like my mind, is completely inflexible.

Today I will share my scattered thoughts by speaking only in sentence fragments, offering no transition statements.

Although deep breathing does calm me, it does not give me the validating and loving attention that hyperventilating and passing out does.

Optimism is for people who can't face the cold, hard reality of life.

Instead of telling myself that I am drowning in debt, I will empower myself by coming to the enlightened viewpoint that I am actually swimming in debt.

Since my gym will not acknowledge that I signed the agreement under duress, and will not give me a refund, this week I will pester them into reconsidering their position.

Today I will attend an aerobics class with a super-sized bag of fast food.

$\mathcal{T}$oday I will reserve the racquetball court and then spend my hour practicing my "dance routine."

$\mathcal{T}$oday I will take binoculars to the gym and blatantly focus on people using the exercise equipment.

$\mathcal{T}$oday I will walk around the gym and tell everyone they're using the equipment improperly.

$\mathcal{T}$oday I will corner people who are alone and say, "Wow, it's really brave of you to come to the gym, considering . . ." and then pat them on the back.

Today I will wear a Walkman to the gym and sing show tunes at the top of my lungs.

∽

Today I will take a puppet to the gym and put on a free show in the locker room.

To save my children from ending up like me, I will employ a team of plastic surgeons and nutritionists to correct their every problem.

Today I will embrace the glorious knowledge that my mistakes have given me. After all, how many people know that cooking wine should never be served chilled?

Since I have no willpower, I will force my family to keep their snack foods in secret places whenever I'm around.

Today I will make a master list of all my other lists so that I can track my every move.

$\mathcal{A}$t the risk of seeming rigid, today I will plan my meals, outfits, and exercise regimes for the next year.

$\mathcal{T}$oday I will make an appointment with myself so that I can explore whether or not I'm self-obsessed.

$\mathcal{G}$oing by all the available charts,
a mammal of my height should
weigh between 100 and 600 pounds.

$\mathcal{I}$ resent when other people attempt
to upstage me by having problems of
their own.

$\mathcal{T}$oday I will practice being a good listener and develop my listening skills by eavesdropping on a private conversation.

$\mathcal{T}$oday I will ask my pharmacist if there is a dual antistretch mark and antifungal cream on the market so that she will have to acknowledge her limited education.

$\mathcal{T}$oday I will satisfy my need to pamper myself by sitting in a chair and barking orders at those around me.

$\mathcal{W}$e've all heard it said that our bodies are temples and should be treated as such. I prefer to think of mine as a strip mall that can provide for some needs but should otherwise be avoided.

As I have very limited skills, my energies would best be utilized for critiquing others.

To accommodate my restricted diet, today I will plan a holiday party at which I will serve only room temperature water.

$\mathcal{T}$oday I will bring a small blanket to work so that when I sneak into the executive bathroom I can nap more peacefully.

୧୨

$\mathcal{T}$oday when I exercise I will visualize frightening scenes such as being mugged so that I can more easily get my heart rate into the "zone."

$\mathcal{I}$'m fairly certain that if my shame didn't prohibit me from putting on a swimsuit, then I would swim regularly for great lengths of time.

$\mathcal{S}$ince I readily accept the fact that I am a materialistic person, I must remember to reward all of my successes, no matter how small, with gigantic, expensive rewards.

$\mathcal{P}$eople who think codependence is unhealthy are merely jealous of the energy and stamina I have when it comes to enabling other people.

$\mathcal{I}$ have often heard that the majority of people do not get enough sleep. This week, I will give myself permission to come to work late every day so that I can be well-rested.

$\mathcal{I}$ have a right not to see my toes . . . or my knees.

Since I cannot trust myself to go to the grocery store and only buy healthful foods, I will petulantly tell friends that if they really cared about me they would do my shopping for me.

On a purely practical level, it is good to be overweight because fat cushions and protects my vital organs.

Stretch marks add variety and texture to my body.

Cigarettes help keep me thin without the bother of exercise.

Although some people seem to disagree, my middle-aged acne proves that I am young at heart.

My large butt has broken many a nasty fall.

❦

I love my light blue eye shadow. Not only does it look really pretty, it shocks people out of noticing the rest of me.

$\mathcal{I}$n order to save the environment, I will not drive to the gym today. I will stay home and eat cold leftovers.

$\mathcal{S}$elf-improvement is actually an insidiously disguised form of denial.

Even though gravity has been unkind to my body, at least everything is sagging in unison.

Nicotine stains give my smile added pizzazz.

Fried foods make me happy. Happy people are beautiful. Therefore, I am beautiful when I eat fried foods.

One's weight should never, ever be higher than, say, one's SAT score.

Today I will remind myself that my pesky body odors prevent unwanted advances as well as sexual harassment.

Thin people bruise far too easily.

$\mathcal{P}$eriodic flatulence is an expressive way to greet the world.

$\mathcal{I}$f the goal of exercise is to increase one's heart rate, then coffee and anxiety allow me to do the same thing without the trouble of changing clothes and showering.

The challenge of tracking down and trimming the unwanted hair growth on my body is a cheap alternative to mystery novels and crossword puzzles.

My gray hairs add body and fullness to my hairstyle.

The true reason that people keep mistaking me for my lover's parent is my maturity.

I like floors to squeak when I step on them. In that way, I can further refine my non-verbal communication skills.

$\mathcal{F}$or this year's swimsuit, I will purchase a body stocking with a supermodel's image on it.

$\mathcal{S}$pandex and lycra should only be used in medical emergencies—as tourniquets.

$\mathcal{M}$y chronic bad breath allows me to keep all conversations short and to the point.

ꙮ

$\mathcal{M}$y hot flashes enable me to experience exotic, tropical climates without the expensive hassle of travel.

Taking so many medications ensures that I always get my eight full glasses of water a day.

My thick glasses have prevented many potentially gruesome eye injuries.

My lengthy bathroom habits allow me to be a voracious reader and, therefore, an educated person.

Liver spots make my pale skin look like it has a healthy glow.

I am proud that my hypochondria subsidizes my doctor's mortgage payments.

I prefer Zen-like stillness and tranquility to maniacal sweating.

Referring to my children as one big hyphenated name proves that I do not have a favorite.

As far as regularity is concerned, fiber has yet to accomplish what simple overeating does.

$\mathcal{M}$y hearing loss enables me to
easily and conveniently tune out
annoying conversations.

$\mathcal{M}$y laziness prevents me from
wandering too far from home.

$\mathcal{I}$ do my part for the economy by constantly purchasing new clothes in the desperate hope—albeit futile—that I will find the magic fit.

$\mathcal{M}$y memory problems enhance my mystique.

$\mathcal{M}$y carefully created and laboriously maintained chapped hands and jagged nails are my best defense against physical contact of any sort.

$\mathcal{I}$ resent that other people's selfishness gets in the way of my narcissism.

In order to shed excess water weight, I will force myself to sleep with an electric blanket set on high all summer.

Because my feelings of self-worth directly correspond to my physical measurements, I will purchase a girdle and a padded, push-up bra today.

Since I hate to see my gym membership go to waste, tonight I will pack my dinner and eat it at the gym.

But I like the way diet pills make me feel. . . . (Read very quickly and repeat incessantly when you're wide awake at 2 AM.)

Although I haven't exercised in years, today I will try to achieve the exercise program of an Olympian.

In order to remind myself how disgusting I think I am, today I will wear dangerously tight clothes that do not allow me to bend any of my joints.

$\mathcal{S}$ince I hate the way I look in a swimsuit, I will wear street clothes to the pool today and "pretend" to fall in.

$\mathcal{A}$lthough experience has taught me that my treadmill makes a fine drying rack, today I will expend my energy searching for an even more creative use for it.

Today I will begin my own twelve-step group. Except there will be thirteen-and-a-half steps and all of them will revolve around me.

So that I can finally know inner happiness, today I will take out a second mortgage on my house in order to finance my extensive plastic surgery.

Although some people caution me about sunbathing, I know they are just jealous that my skin feels like a really expensive, Italian purse.

After spending all day yesterday at the mall, today I'm going to call the police on the circus freak who stalked me in all the dressing rooms and appeared in all the mirrors.

Today I will ignore all of my physical
needs, no matter how persistent
they are.

Although some may say that my
plastic surgeon really botched my
face-lift, I like looking continually
surprised. It makes my friends and
family believe I'm happy to see them.

$\mathcal{T}$oday I will find "proof" for all my whacked-out health theories from shady sources on the Internet.

$\mathcal{I}$n order to win my family's sympathy, I will act as if I am anorexic at our next holiday meal.

$\mathcal{T}$his year I will quantify everything in my life, ranking my friends and family according to their score.

$\mathcal{I}$ am not high-maintenance.
I simply have more necessities than most people.

Tomorrow at work, I will call out the caloric value of foods I see people eating.

After acclimating my coworkers to my bizarre, verbal calorie counting, I will begin to undermine those thinner than me by calling out purposely deflated estimates.

$\mathcal{I}$ may as well face the fact that entire cities are maintained at less cost and with less effort than it takes me to groom myself.

$\mathcal{T}$oday I will eat a huge serving of beans before going to my yoga class.

$\mathcal{M}$y wonderfully honed procrastination skills ensure that I will never run out of self-improvement projects.

$\mathcal{T}$oday I will poison my innate healer.

The next time I eat out I will make it a point to complain loudly about how fattening restaurant food is.

I really resent that other walkers stare at me simply because I use a suitcase on wheels instead of a fanny pack.

Since I hate physical contact, the next time someone wants a hug, I will "pretend" to mishear them and offer them a bug.

Today I will buy more plastic cockroaches.

The next time I trip over what can only be described as an air molecule, I will pretend to be having a back spasm rather than admit my inherent clumsiness.

The next time I pull a muscle doing something ordinary—like picking up the morning newspaper—I will tell everyone I hurt myself while training for my first marathon.

If one size truly does fit all, then theoretically I wear the same size as a supermodel.

Instead of indulging the ingrates in my family with more costly birthday gifts, I will treat myself to a weekend at a spa and send them postcards.

This year, I will concentrate on the language I use to describe myself, making sure to include words such as fatty, droopy, and frumpy.

In order to prepare for the new millennium, I will allow myself to order as many exercise gizmos as I want—no matter how hokey.

The next time I am in a bad mood I will write angry notes to everyone and anyone who has annoyed me to even the slightest degree.

Because I am prone to eating fast foods when I'm on the go, I will now plan ahead and keep candy bars in my glove compartment.

$\mathcal{P}$eople often say I'm opinionated because they obviously cannot comprehend the depth of my knowledge and wisdom.

$\mathcal{T}$his month I will join as many churches/synagogues/mosques as possible so that I can reap the benefits of joining a singles network without the humiliation.

$\mathcal{I}$f one is supposed to wear loose-fitting clothing while exercising, then why don't athletic clothes manufacturers make caftans?

$\mathcal{I}$n order to avoid eating too much junk food at the next party I attend, I will begin dancing as soon as I arrive, whether there's music playing or not.

The next time I go on vacation
I will take my own scale as a guilty
reminder of how unhappy I am with
my body.

Because I hate vacationing with
my family, this year I will organize a
disastrously boring camping trip as a
way of terminating this ill-conceived
tradition.

$\mathcal{I}$'m worried that my tendency to second-guess myself is precluding my progress. Maybe I'm wrong . . . but then again. . . .

$\mathcal{T}$he next time I host a party, I will ask people to bring household items that I need instead of food.

$\mathcal{T}$his week I will join a walking club at the local mall as a covert way to indulge my compulsive shopping habits.

$\mathcal{T}$oday I will purchase an air horn so that I can set it off the next time I am presented with a temptation, thus scaring away the evil people who are trying to lure me off my path to perfection.

Today I will call my doctor to discuss my suspicion that I am actually allergic to whole grains, fruits, and vegetables.

The next time someone complains that I gave them a gift I really wanted for myself, I will explain that I'm simply living by the golden rule.

Since true contentment and peace come from within, from now on I will give up my ridiculously futile habit of housecleaning to pursue this goal.

Today I will go to the bank and apply for a loan. I will tell the loan officer that I need it because I am completely and utterly out of control with my money.

$\mathcal{T}$he next time someone shares their stress with me I will attempt to calm them down by explaining in detail the threats of stress on the heart.

$\mathcal{I}$ would find it much easier to enjoy nature if it weren't so wild and unorganized.

$\mathcal{B}$ecause my life is so intricate and complex, it is so much more difficult for me to accomplish my goals.

$\mathcal{T}$oday I will besmirch my essential beauty.

$\mathcal{I}$f only I would have started all my self-improvement regimes years ago, I would have already reached my goals by now.

$\mathcal{S}$ince I highly doubt there is any power greater than myself, I will focus all my energies on gaining power over as many others as possible.

$\mathcal{T}$oday I will publicly take responsibility for my personal resentments by writing an open letter to the newspaper.

$\mathcal{A}$s proof of my strength, today I will cling tenaciously to an outdated and self-destructive belief about myself, despite mounting evidence to the contrary.

$\mathcal{I}$ feel content with the fact that my fear of success and my fear of failure keep me on an even keel in this chaotic world.

$\mathcal{T}$oday I will visualize myself designing a map so that I can navigate the rest of my life without making mistakes, taking detours, and falling behind.

$\mathcal{T}$oday I will remind myself that failure is final. Once I have screwed up, I might as well give up completely on that goal and move to the next.

$\mathcal{T}$his year I will struggle to accept my inability to accept myself.

Since I hate solitude and reflective thought, I will be sure that this year's calendar is crowded with deadlines, inked-in plans, and goals.

The next time someone tries to take my picture, I will purposefully place myself next to someone less attractive than I am—even if I have to pull an absolute stranger into the photo.

Although others often characterize me as bitter and hostile, I am actually a very nice person who just happens to be hungry from constant dieting.

Since I am obviously incapable of changing myself, my only choice is to change everything and everyone around me to adapt to my specific and unusual needs.

As so many people accuse me of being too perfect, today I will pick up some bad habits just to prove them wrong.

The fact that I've had to start over so many times is proof that I shouldn't be making my own decisions.

For their birthday presents, I will buy my friends self-improvement books about issues I think they need to deal with, highlighting the especially relevant sections.

If anyone communicates so much as even the tiniest disappointment over my gift selection, I will nod patronizingly, pat them on the back and absentmindedly comment about the horrors of denial.

$\mathcal{I}$n order to control my eating, I will no longer allow myself to snack while showering.

$\mathcal{T}$oday I will practice being assertive using a mirror. In order to use the energy I expend doing this more efficiently, I will carry the mirror in my pocket and allow myself to use it in public.

$\mathcal{T}$oday I will grade everything I do in a harsh and defeatist manner.

$\mathcal{E}$ven though my doctor vehemently denies it, I know in my heart that my insomnia-induced tossing and turning is a legitimate form of exercise.

$\mathcal{T}$he true direction of my life is too complex to reveal to others.

$\mathcal{M}$y difficulty waking up in the morning is reason enough for me to always be in a "serious relationship." After all, I know from experience that human alarm clocks work best.

$\mathcal{A}$lthough some people accuse me of acting superior to others, the plain truth of the matter is that I am superior.

$\mathcal{I}$ am very pleased that my intentionally pervasive and disgusting body odor effectively stops people from noticing my professional incompetence.

Since anger and shame have failed as motivational tools in the past, today I shall cultivate feelings of envy to achieve my goals.

After recognizing my sexual conduct for the misguided and misdirected behavior it is, I can now move to the next step of the process: rationalizing it and making excuses.

$\mathcal{B}$ecause I hate taking a stand, this year I will practice making all my opinions so diplomatic that they are actually meaningless babble.

$\mathcal{T}$his year I will refine my phone screening techniques so that I can more convincingly ignore my needy friends while appearing to be supportive.

$\mathcal{I}$n order to safeguard my free time, today I will accuse my friends of holding me hostage to their obviously unsolved childhood issues.

$\mathcal{S}$ince everyone knows a positive attitude contributes to good health, this year I will make it a point to avoid all friends and family members who are going through hard times.

$\mathcal{A}$ll my dreams, goals, and aspirations have died. Today I will bury them in the backyard and force my friends to attend the ceremony.

$\mathcal{B}$ecause I believe my boss has unrealistically high expectations, today I will earn a well-deserved break by causing a huge interoffice drama that brings all work to a complete standstill.

Since all the petty people at my office make me look like I take too many coffee breaks, I will secretly pull the fire alarm today so that I can enjoy the fresh air without appearing unproductive.

I must remember to count the twenty-five flights of steps I walked down today during the fire drill as the physical exercise that it was.

$\mathcal{I}$n order to better indulge my innate cowardice, today I will deflect all attention and shirk all responsibilities.

$\mathcal{I}$ am proud that my ability to deceive myself is surpassed only by my ability to deceive others.

Since I have spent most of my life being a sniveling, pathetic victim, it is okay for me to be a bully now.

Today I will actualize my repressed ogre.

$\mathcal{T}$oday I will begin a list of all the things in my life that I hate, so that tomorrow I can completely avoid each one.

∞

$\mathcal{T}$oday I will thwart the efforts of others to lose weight by taking a particularly delicious food-scented air freshener to a weight-loss meeting.

Since most people are not trustworthy, today I will work on devising a plan to statistically "test" my friends' trustworthiness and loyalty.

Because I despise physical contact, the next time someone bumps into me I will launch into a series of "original" karate moves complete with guttural noises.

$\mathcal{P}$eople who prattle on endlessly about the importance of mental health simply cannot deal with how liberating strategically used neurosis can be.

$\mathcal{S}$ince my own appearance is in shambles, this year I will compensate by beautifying my pets.

$\mathcal{I}$n order to better nurture my
inherently argumentative nature,
today I will start all of my sentences
with the words "Yes, but . . ."

$\mathcal{S}$ince I am having difficulty
using alternative techniques of self–
improvement, today I will visualize
myself doing visualization. The next
day I will move on to the actual
visualization.

The next time someone tells me I don't have a sense of humor I will point out how easily I laugh at others.

Today I will celebrate my ability to resist change and regress to old, obnoxious patterns of behavior.

$\mathcal{T}$he whole concept of "letting go" is for people who don't have the spiritual and emotional strength to hold on to things.

$\mathcal{S}$ince it is impossible for me to admit when I'm wrong, I will systematically and succinctly cut people out of my life who expect me to do so.

$\mathcal{I}$ must remember to put my food diary next to my bed so that I can enter all my snacks.

$\mathcal{I}$n order to get the extended paid vacation that I alone am entitled to, today I will alternate between weeping and threatening people with pepper spray at work.

$\mathcal{S}$ince I have so little tolerance for other people's flaws, today I will isolate myself in my own little world of perfection and illusion.

$\mathcal{M}$y ability to think in sweeping and ungrounded generalizations proves that I'm a philosophically oriented person, not the superficial fiend I'm often accused of being.

$\mathcal{B}$ecause I can only achieve results through competition, today I will start a weight-loss contest with a friend.

$\mathcal{B}$ecause I have an inalienable right to win every competition, I will rig the initial weigh-in by duct taping small but heavy objects to my body, concealing them with baggy clothes.

Since I am trying to achieve balance in my life, today I will watch one hour of TV for every hour I spend at work.

In order to keep those around me on their toes, today I will make an effort to display inappropriate reactions to even the smallest requests.

$\mathcal{T}$his week I will engage people by smiling and then deliberately confuse them by saying only venomous things.

$\mathcal{T}$oday I will act on a destructive impulse.

$\mathcal{T}$o ensure that I achieve serenity,
I must remember to stop the anxiety-producing behavior of challenging myself.

$\mathcal{I}$n order to increase my chances
at material and worldly success,
I must remember to add prayer to
my repertoire of sabotage and
underhandedness.

*I*nstead of second-guessing myself today, I will verbally encourage others to do so by asking, "Are you sure?" about everything.

*T*he fact that "one size fits all" clothing does not fit me proves that I am, somehow, grossly misshapen.

$\mathcal{T}$oday I will graciously forgive someone who is angry with me by starting the conversation with "I forgive you."

$\mathcal{S}$o that I can prove to others how truly flexible I am, today I will count potato chips as my vegetable servings and strawberry ice cream as my fruit servings.

In order to achieve perfect health, today I will employ my consumerist techniques by purchasing vitamins and supplements. Later today, I will allow myself to not take them for fear of side effects.

Failure is not a destination but a journey.

$\mathcal{T}$oday I will allow myself to fall peacefully into sleep while watching my favorite exercise video.

$\mathcal{D}$o you have a cynical affirmation
you would like to share?

If so, send it to:

Sarah Wells and Ann Thornhill
C/O Prima Publishing
P.O. Box 1260 Martyr
Rocklin, CA 95677

Please note: Prima Publishing may want to publish
your cynical affirmation along with your name in a
future version of this book. By submitting a response,
you agree that Prima shall own all rights to publish
the affirmation and give credit to you as the author
of the affirmation.